THE BOOK OF FECKIN' IRISH INSULTS

FOR GOBDAWS AS THICK AS MANURE AND ONLY HALF AS USEFUL

THE BOOK OF FECKIN' IRISH INSULTS FOR GOBDAWS AS THICK AS MANURE AND ONLY HALF AS USEFUL

Colin Murphy & Donal O'Dea

THE O'BRIEN PRESS
DUBLIN

This revised edition first published 2019 by
The O'Brien Press Ltd,
12 Terenure Road East, Rathgar, Dublin 6, D06 HD27, Ireland.
Tel: +353 1 4923333; Fax: +353 1 4922777
E-mail: books@obrien.ie
Website: www.obrien.ie
First published 2006.
Reprinted 2007, 2009, 2011, 2012, 2014, 2017.
The O'Brien Press is a member of Publishing Ireland.

ISBN: 978-1-78849-169-3

23 22 21 20 19
6 5 4 3 2 1

Printed and bound by Gutenberg Press, Malta.
The paper used in this book is produced using pulp from
managed forests.

Published in

DUBLIN
UNESCO
City of Literature

Any friend of yours is a friend of yours.

You are a gobshite, as is anyone associated with you.

As fat as a Galway bishop.

Overweight. (Possibly conceived with the generously proportioned and amorous Bishop Casey in mind.)

MICK'S AS FAT AS A GALWAY BISHOP.

YEAH, HE EATS AND DRINKS RELIGIOUSLY.

A sharp tongue doesn't mean she has a keen mind.

She's a stupid bitch.

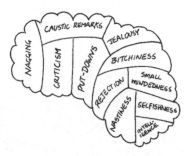

Asking her who's the father would be like asking which bean caused the fart.

She's of loose virtue.

As tight as a nun's knickers.
He's a stingy bastard.

As useful as a chocolate teapot.
Utterly useless.

As useful as a
concrete currach.
Completely useless.

As useful as an ashtray
in a force 10 gale.
Absolutely useless.

As useful as a one-legged man in an arse-kicking contest.

Totally useless.

For someone without any cows, he produces an awful lot of bullshit.

All talk, no substance.

God used him as the blueprint for a gobshite.

He is the mother of all gobshites.

Go on home and tell your oul' wan to get married.

You're a bastard.

He cheats when filling out opinion polls.

He is a moron of the first degree.

He couldn't hit sand if he fell off a camel.

His aim is brutal.

11

He couldn't pick the winner of a one-horse race.

His judgment is utterly crap.

He doesn't know his arse from his elbow.

He is clueless in all things.

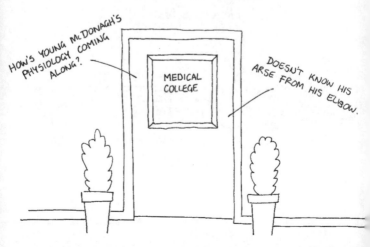

He'd live in your left ear and grow spuds in your right.

He's a stingy gobshite.

He'd shite in your parlour and charge you for it.

He's not only ignorant, but stingy to boot.

He'd steal the eye outta yer head and come back for the lashes.

He's a chancer and a layabout.

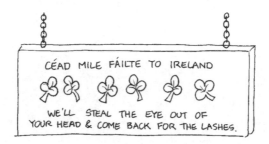

He'd wring drink out of a floozie's knickers.

He will go to any lengths to acquire alcohol (esp. for free)

He got out of the wrong side of the cage this morning.

*Not only is he an ignorant pig,
he's also in a lousy mood.*

He had a face on him as long as a donkey's back leg.

He is a dour gobshite.

He has a face like a constipated greyhound.

He is in a wojus humour.

He has a face like the divil's arse.

He is in an extremely angry and agitated state.

He has a face on him as long as a wet week in February.

He has an excessively melancholic puss on him.

He has a head on him like a bulldog licking piss off a nettle.

He is an ugly gouger.

He has an arsehole at both ends of his digestive system.
He is an unpleasant bowsie who frequently talks bullshit.

He has a photographic memory, but there's no film in the camera.
He is a complete eejit.

He has the attention span of a bag of spuds.

He is a total moron.

He has trouble spelling IQ.

He is an utter gobdaw.

	IQ RATING		
170+	GENIUS	80	BELOW AVERAGE INTELLIGENCE
150	V. INTELLIGENT	70	STUPID
130	INTELLIGENT	60	COMPLETE MORON
100	BRIGHT	50	GOVERNMENT MINISTER

He is the sap in the family tree.
In terms of intelligence, he is the black sheep of the family.

Her arse is as wide as a Leitrim hurler's shot.
She has excessively broad buttocks.

He reminds me of the Irish sea
... he makes me sick.

He is a nauseating bowsie.

He was born a day late and
he's been like that ever since.

He is an unreliable and unpunctual skiver.

He was premature at birth and has the same problem at conception.

He is lousy in the scratcher.

He'll be late for his own funeral.

He is a brutal timekeeper.

Her looks improve with distance.
She is an ugly wagon.

MISS IRELAND 1960	MISS IRELAND 1970	MISS IRELAND 1980	MISS IRELAND 1990	MISS IRELAND 2000	MISS IRELAND 2006

0	20	40	60	80	100

← METRES →

Her mind wandered and never came home.
She is a thick wagon.

SORRY, MY MIND WAS WANDERING.

WONDER IF IT EVER FOUND ITS WAY HOME?

Her weighing scale reads 'one at a time, please.'

She's a gluttonous wagon.

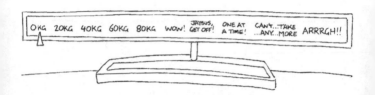

He's a complete waste of space.

He has absolutely no redeeming characteristics.

He's a few cans short
of a six-pack.

He's a bit of a mentaller.

He's a few eggs short
of a basket.

He's a tad nuts.

He's a few pints short
of a milk churn.
He's a complete lune.

He's a neck
like a jockey's bollox.
*He is thick-skinned and doesn't care
what others think of him.*

He sank in the gene pool.

*Genetically speaking, he is a thick,
ignorant sleeveen.*

He's as agile as a one-armed
man climbing a rope.

He is a clumsy gobshite.

He's as ignorant
as a sack of arses.

*He is a gouger completely lacking
in the social graces.*

He's as sharp as a hurley.

He's a thick gobshite.

He's like a pig knitting.
*He is an awkward eejit, physically,
socially, or both.*

He's nobody's fool – he can't
get anyone to adopt him.
He's an eejit.

He's so boring that he can't even entertain an idea.

He's a dry shite, to be avoided socially at all cost.

He's the world's first experiment in artificial stupidity.

He's a moronic gobdaw.

He supplies the entire town
with natural gas.
He has uncontrollable flatulence.

He tries to be a wit but he's
only halfway there.
He is excessively dense.

He wouldn't give you the steam off his piss.

He's a stingy bowsie.

He wouldn't know his langer from his thumb except for the nail.

He hasn't a clue how to interact with women, even those of loose virtue.

His brain has gone home but his gob's working overtime.

He is talking bullshit.

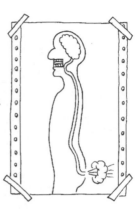

AS YOU CAN SEE FROM THIS X RAY, THE CONNECTION FROM YOUR BRAIN TO YOUR MOUTH HAS SOMEHOW GOT MIXED UP WITH THE ONE TO YOUR RECTUM. WHICH EXPLAINS WHY YOU'RE TALKING THROUGH YOUR ARSE...

His head's as big as Malin Head.

He's a gobshite who admires himself too much.

HEY, BABE. I'M THE MAN OF YOUR DREAMS

DID YOU KNOW THE SIZE OF A MAN'S HEAD IS DISPROPORTIONATE TO HIS PENIS?

His idea of helping with the housework is lifting his feet so you can vacuum.

He's a lazy, skiving dosser.

His lift doesn't go all the way to the top floor.

He's a poor thick eejit.

His mind is so open that ideas simply pass through it.

He's an absolute moron.

I bet your brain feels as good as new, seeing that you've never used it.

Mentally, you're a lazy gobdaw.

If brains were taxed, he'd be due a rebate.

He's an imbecile.

If bullshit was music, he'd be a céilí band.

He's a blatherer of the highest order.

I don't think you're a gobshite, but what's my opinion compared to thousands of others?

Everyone you know believes you to be a bowsie and a shitehawk.

OPINION POLLS LTD.

Q: HOW WOULD YOU DESCRIBE THE CURRENT CABINET ?

HONEST
HARDWORKING
EFFECTIVE
BUNCH OF GOBSHITES

If he went any slower he'd catch up with himself on the way back.

He's a painfully slow mover.

CIVIL SERVICE

JOB INTERVIEWS TODAY

MR RICE, YOU ARRIVED 30 MINUTES LATE, IT TOOK YOU 2 HOURS TO FILL OUT THE FORM, YOU SHOW NO APTITUDE FOR ANYTHING. YOU'RE LAZY, UNAMBITIOUS AND YOU HAVE NO MANNERS. YOU'RE PERFECT FOR THE JOB.

If ignorance is bliss, she must be the happiest person alive.
She's a thick skanger.

If she ever breastfeeds, the baby will end up malnourished.
She has microscopically small boobs.

If work was a bed he'd sleep on the floor.

He is a total dosser.

I hear he was born on a farm. There were six in the litter.

He's a manky pig.

I'm not saying he's dense, but he stared at a carton of orange juice for 20 minutes because it said 'concentrate' on the label.

He's a fierce eejit.

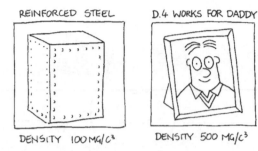

I'm not saying she's thick, but when there's a wind blowing her head whistles.

She's a stupid wagon.

Irish men are like bottles of stout – empty from the neck up.

Irish men are thoughtless gobshites.

I see your mother knows which sexual position produces the ugliest children.

You're an ugly geebag/gouger.

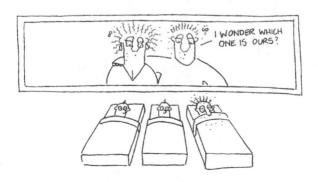

**It's hard to see his point of
view, as most people can't get
their head that far up their
own arse.**

You're a self-obsessed sleeveen.

**It's not so much he's not
playing with a full deck, more
like he's not even in the game.**

Not only is he dense, he's a bit of a lune.

I wouldn't cross Leeson Street to piss on him if his jocks were on fire.

He's a total gouger.

Missing a few sheep from her flock.

She's a bit of a nut case.

Modesty suits him perfectly.
He has no redeeming features.

Mother Nature hates him – he reminds her of her mistakes.
He is an utter gobshite.

My car has five airbags – at least when my mother-in-law is a passenger.
My mother-in-law is an absolute wagon.

Next time you might be reincarnated as a human.
You're a complete pig.

She'd talk the teeth off a saw.

She never shuts her gob.

She fell into a pot of jam and had to eat her way out.

She's a slapper who wears too much make-up.

She has a face like a
bag of spanners.
She is hideously ugly.

She has a face like the
back of a turf cart.
She is physically repulsive.

She has a face on her as long as a horse's arse.

She is a sullen geebag.

She has a face on her that would turn milk.

She has an incredibly sour puss/incredibly ugly puss.

She has a face that'd
stop a clock.
She is incredibly ugly.

She has a head on her
like a slapped arse.
*She is a brutal-looking,
red-complexioned wagon.*

She has an arse on her like a brewery drayhorse.

She has a colossal arse.

She's a few carrots short of a stew.

She's a bit crazy.

She's a few screams
short of an orgasm.
She's a little nuts/lousy in bed.

She's a product
tester for Viagra.
She's a scanger who sleeps around.

She's a walking argument for contraception.

She's a horrible geebag.

She's as beautiful as a TD is honest.

She is the ugliest person on the planet.

She's as exciting as a wet night in Athlone.

She's a boring wagon.

She's bound to meet some good-looking, successful genius. After all, don't opposites attract?

She is a repulsive, thick failure.

She's immune to brain damage.
She's thick.

She's not completely useless – she's a life-support system for a fanny.
She's an idiot but reputedly good in the scratcher.

She's like a bag of cats thrun into a bonfire.

She's a bad-humoured fecker.

She's not so much an oil painting as a mosaic.

Her complexion is brutal/she's ancient.

She's overdue
for reincarnation.
She's a gobshite.

She's so boring
she makes onions cry.
She's a terrible dry shite.

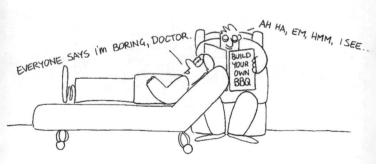

She's so fat she comes from both sides of the family tree.

She's horribly overweight.

She's so skinny she can dodge raindrops.

She's anorexically thin.

She's so stupid she spells farm E-I-E-I-O.
She's an incredibly stupid yoke.

She's so thick she tried to put a fish out of its misery by drowning it.
She's a moron.

She's such a bad cook,
she even makes a pig's dinner
of feeding the pigs.

She's a lousy cook.

ACTUALLY, LOVE, I THINK YOU'LL FIND THE "BANGERS" IN "BANGERS AND MASH" USUALLY MEANS SAUSAGES.

She's the width of
a Mullingar heifer.

She has a huge arse.

THEY'RE DOING LIPOSUCTION ON BIDDY MAGUIRE AGAIN.

CLINIC

She was never given the bad taste vaccine in school.

She dresses like a slapper.

That fella'd skin a fart.

He's a bowsie who'd do anything for money.

The good Lord used him for miracle practice.

He's an ugly, stupid fecker.

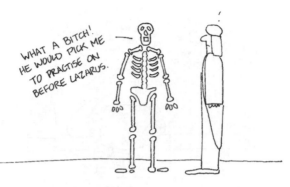

We all spring from apes, but he didn't spring far enough.

He's an uncouth gouger.

When he was born, his mother throw rocks at the stork.

He is physically repugnant.

When she walks into a room, the mice jump on chairs.

She is physically repugnant.

You big long mother's rarin'!

You are a total mammy's boy.

THE BIG LONG MOTHER'S RARIN' COULDN'T EVEN BLOW OUT ALL THE CANDLES HIS MAMMY GOT FOR HIS CAKE....

HOW MANY WERE THERE?

47.

You smell like a slapper's handbag.
You are wearing excessive amounts of cheap perfume.

SLAPPER'S HANDBAG OFFICIAL CONTENTS GUIDE

L'EAU DE VALUESHOP x3

BOTTLE MASCARA

POWDER COMPACT

€200 FOR DRINK

RIBBED CONDOMS x30

RED LIPSTICK x 2

BOTTLE RED NAIL VARNISH

SPARE EARRINGS (IN CASE ONE GETS TORN OFF IN A FIGHT)

OLD FAG ENDS x6

SPARE KNICKERS x 4

Despite being the co-author of a hugely successful series of books on aspects of Irish culture, COLIN MURPHY regularly has a face on him like a constipated greyhound. It is widely known that he'd wring drink out of a floozie's knickers yet is as tight as a nun's drawers. His normal employment involves writing ads, which is just as well, because if bullshit was music, he'd be a céilí band. When he was born, his mother threw rocks at the stork, which makes the fact that he is married with two teenage kids all the more amazing. His one redeeming feature is that his looks improve with distance.

DONAL O'DEA is a very modest man, which is fortunate as modesty suits him perfectly. Despite having reaped the rewards of being the Feckin' books co-author, he'd still live in your left ear and grow spuds in your right. By day he's an art director in a leading Irish ad agency, something at which he's as useful as an ashtray in a force 10 gale. By night he drinks so much he becomes as ignorant as a sack of arses. His idea of helping with the housework is lifting his feet so his wife can vacuum and even his three kids think he's a few cans short of a six-pack.

PES THE BOOK OF FECKIN' IRISH SAYINGS
ECKIN' IRISH TRIVIA THE FECKIN' BOOK (
 FECKIN' IRISH BOOK THE FECKIN' BOOK
 THE FECKIN' BOOK OF IRISH STUFF WHO
IN' LIKE A MASSIVE BOOK OF FECKIN' IRI
BOWSIES THE BOOK OF FECKIN' IRISH S
BOOK OF FECKIN' IRISH SONGS THE BO(
IN' IRISH RECIPES THE BOOK OF FECKI
LTS THE BOOK OF FECKIN' IRISH TRIVIA
'S WHAT I CALL A BIG FECKIN' IRISH B(
IN' BOOK OF IRISH LOVE THE FECKIN' BO
ORY WHAT ARE WE FECKIN' LIKE A MAS
ECKIN' IRISH BANKERS AND BOWSIES TI
IN' IRISH QUOTATIONS THE BOOK OF FE
& LOVE THE BOOK OF FECKIN' IRISH RE(
K OF FECKIN' IRISH INSULTS THE BOOK
YTHING IRISH NOW THAT'S WHAT I CALL
 HISTORY THE FECKIN' BOOK OF IRISH
IN' WHO IN IRISH HISTORY WHAT ARE WE
G THE BOOK OF FECKIN' IRISH BANKERS
BOOK OF FECKIN' IRISH QUOTATIONS TI
IN' IRISH SEX & LOVE THE BOOK OF FE(
NGS THE BOOK OF FECKIN' IRISH INSULT